BLACK GLASS

BLACK GLASS

NEW AND SELECTED POEMS

Wayne Burrows

Shoestring Press

All rights reserved. No part of this work covered by the copyright hereon may be reproduced or used in any means – graphic, electronic, or mechanical, including copying, recording, taping, or information storage and retrieval systems – without written permission of the publisher.

Printed by imprintdigital
Upton Pyne, Exeter
www.imprintdigital.net

Typeset by narrator
www.narrator.me.uk
info@narrator.me.uk
033 022 300 39

Published by Shoestring Press
19 Devonshire Avenue, Beeston, Nottingham, NG9 1BS
(0115) 925 1827
www.shoestringpress.co.uk

First published 2015
© Copyright: Wayne Burrows

The moral right of the author has been asserted.

ISBN 978-1-910323-25-0

Acknowledgements

Some of these poems, or versions of them, first appeared in *Marginalia* (Peterloo Poets, 2001), *Emblems* (Shoestring Press, 2009), *Said and Done* (Stonewood Press, 2010), *The Apple Sequence* (Orchard Editions, 2011), *The Thread* (Nottingham Contemporary, 2011), *Poetry Review, Poetry Wales, Brittle Star, Vanguard Poetry, Fit To Work: Poets Against ATOS* and *LeftLion*. 'On A Very Small Planet, Not Too Far Away' was first published as a poetry card by Shoestring Press in 2013.

'The Protein Songs', 'That Afternoon' and 'Siesta Hour' were developed through a commission from Filip Van Huffel and Natalie Gordon at Retina Dance Company to write in response to the theme of 'the body'. Early versions appeared in the tour programme of the UK and European performances of *Eleven Stories For The Body, Distance To Our Soul* (Retina Dance Company, 2005).

The Apple Sequence was first published as part of Neville Gabie's *Orchard*, a series of commissions funded by the European Union and Nottingham City Council, managed by Contemporary Art Society, curator Jennie Syson and Patel Taylor Architects, based in a historic fruit and vegetable market on the east side of Nottingham's city centre. 'A Grubbed Orchard (Does Spring Come?)' by Yi Sang-hwa is freely adapted from a version in Peter H. Lee (ed.): *Poems from Korea: from the Earliest Era to the Present Day* (George Allen & Unwin/UNESCO, 1974).

'By Way of Digression...' was commissioned by Nottingham Contemporary as a response to the Frances Stark exhibition *But What of Frances Stark, Standing By Itself, A Naked Name* (2009) while 'Zeropolis, or Shelley in Las Vegas', 'Sonnets in the Aftermath and Anticipation of a Financial Meltdown' and an early version of 'Black Glass' were developed during a *Write Here* residency, jointly funded by Nottingham Contemporary and Writing East Midlands, in Spring 2011.

'The Shadow' is a free adaptation of the Welsh *hen benillion* folk verse 'Angau', first drawn to my attention by Ceridwen Lloyd

Morgan. Various sources have been used, including 'Death', a 1944 version from *The Welsh Review* included by Gwyn Jones in *The Oxford Book of Welsh Verse in English* (OUP, 1977). 'After Englynion' and 'Stanzas for the Harp' also draw on some material from this source.

Two lines in 'The Blue Wolves And The Wheelbarrow' are direct quotation from Eva Švankmajerová, *I Don't Know Exactly*, as translated by Katerina Piňosová in *Surrealist Women: An International Anthology*, ed. Penelope Rosemont (Athlone Press, 1998).

'Panis et Circensis (Bread and Circuses)' is freely adapted from the Portuguese lyric of a song written by Gilberto Gil and Caetano Veloso, originally released in Brazil on the LP *Tropicália: ou Panis et Circensis* (1968) in a version performed by Os Mutantes.

"Luigi Russolo" by Alan Dixon (see p. 79)

Contents

from Marginalia (2001)	1
Llanddwyn	3
After Englynion	4
Binary	6
A Recipe for Insanity	7
Stanzas for the Harp	9
Transference	13
Marginalia	14
The Bubble	15
from The Protein Songs (2005)	17
The Protein Songs	19
That Afternoon	24
Siesta Hour	25
from Emblems (2009)	29
A Trick Of The Light	31
Slapstick (Coda)	32
The Archway Altarpiece	33
Side-Effects	34
Underground	35
from The Apple Sequence (2011)	37
The Apple Prologue	39
The Apple Migrations	41
The Roots of the Apple	44
(i) East Malling, 1912	44
(ii) Herefordshire, 2011	45
Egremont Russet	46
James Grieve	47

Hidden Rose	48
Newton's Wonder	49
The Apple's Song in Autumn	50
Things That Are Not Apples	51
A Grubbed Orchard (Does Spring Come...?)	53
The Order of Seasons	55

Uncollected Poems (2006 – 2014)   59

Lines after Abbas Ibn Al-Ahnaf	61
The Blue Wolves and the Wheelbarrow	62
Black Glass	65
Zeropolis, or Shelley in Las Vegas	68
Instructions for Baking the Nottingham Golem	70
A Simultaneous Translation (April 10, 2013)	72
The Second Time as Farce	77
Luigi Russolo	79
The Shadow	81
By Way of Digression	83
Mnemonic to Aid Understanding of Public Debate Concerning the Fiscal Deficit	85
Sonnets in the Aftermath and Anticipation of a Financial Meltdown	86
(i) Genesis	86
(ii) The Commandments	87
(iii) A Prayer	88
(iv) Revelation	89
On A Very Small Planet, Not Too Far Away	90

A Cycle of Songs from the Body's Interior   93

Panis et Circensis (Bread and Circuses)	95
(i) The Leukocytes	96
(ii) The History of the Red Cells	96
(iii) The Origin of the Heart Beat	96
(iv) Electrical Changes in the Heart	97

(v) Perfusion of the Excised Heart	97
(vi) The Circulation	98
(vii) Skin Sensations	98
(viii) The Lachrymal Apparatus	99
(ix) The Properties of Nerve	99
(x) Nerve Regeneration	100
(xi) The Peripheral Nerves	100
(xii) The Endocrine System	100
(xiii) The Semicircular Canals	101
(xiv) The Primary Organs of Sex	101
(xv) The Physiology of Reproduction	102
(xvi) Pregnancy and Parturition	103
(xvii) The Quadrants of the Breast	103
(xviii) The Deep Layers	104
(xix) The Arterial Pulse	104
(xx) The Cortical Structures	105
(xxi) Examination of the Tongue	105
(xxii) Supplementary Physical Signs	106
(xxiii) The Degeneration of Tissue	106
(xxiv) Disorders of the Heart	106
(xxv) The Coats of the Eye Ball	107

from *Marginalia* (2001)

Llanddwyn

(after Pennar Davies)

Let us now stand here, glance
through light as it enters the shallows
and shows the sun and water fused;
let us seize what their coupling
reveals to us, hold in mind
how its sparkling pewter-white
turns gold, copulates with slate-blue waves,
surges, laps around our feet
and foams where salt water ovulates stones
in the lime-washed force-field
of the daylight moon. It exults
in our presence, reels at the touch
of our eyes on its skin, not living,
as we are, but nonetheless
with a kind of life. It is blur
and motion, wash and heave,
where the sun's tumescence attains
its height. Let us rejoice,
beloved, as water-sparks
flower in the reed-beds. Let us be flooded,
exorcised of all our doubt,
connected to gulls swooping low in the light,
to the herring-shoal. Let the play
of warmth on sunlit waves bring rabbits
tumbling from the warren-mouth.
All brims over like a wooden bowl
in sudden rain, its meaning
ours, ourselves its source, from ocean
to estuary, cloudscape, land,
nothing set apart from us,
from shamelessness, till we cease
to look, or lack joy in love.

After Englynion

What's this odd, loping beast, Idwal?
It's neither insect, fowl nor fish;
a chicken's body on the feet of an eel
or an englyn written in English?

(after Waldo Williams)

(i)

A mattress of heather, sprung on ochre ground,
clings to the rock like a peal of bells;
on the harshest plateaux of sun and wind
these flowers of stone yield honey-phials.

(after Eifion Wyn)

(ii)

Geese break the mirrored skin of the lake,
scatter across the dawn like seed;
when nightfall stumbles on the slippery rock
they sprout, and flower in a honking cloud.

(after Euros Bowen)

(iii)

The ocean sweeps from the beach and spreads
the white lace hem of its silver skirt;
cold rocks tease out its glittering threads
on a curving shore, under failing light.

(after Roland John)

(iv)

Echoed in the mouths of the silenced dead
constellations gleam in these overhangs;
where acres of fish slip nets of weed
oysters balance white pearls on tongues.

   (after R. Williams Parry)

(v)

Silence travels with the dark at night
and the mountain sounds, awash with leaves;
the sun sleeps soundly on a bed of salt
while the moon lies shivering in the waves.

   (after Gwallter Mechain)

(vi)

The night swings open on a hinge of stars,
one star remaining, like a compass-point;
at the door, the candle you hold to your face
is fixed as a nail-head, and radiant.

   (after Coslett Coslett)

(vii)

Rain steams, thickening its muffled noise
to a thousand cramped in a milking byre;
when the slate roof's frozen, thatched with ice,
cold teats, the colour of milk, appear.

   (after Ellis Jones)

Binary

She is dreaming water, her skin turned cold
as gelatine, her body a flickering
translucency barely clear of the air
it breathes. She is all reflection
and play of light, her voice a wave-form
more felt than heard. If she crosses darkness
like a jellyfish or lens escaped
from a microscope, she'll move unseen.
When she wakes, she'll wake to rain on glass,
his face in the mirror. *A veil of breath.*

A Recipe for Insanity

Imagine the earth as it spins through space
so fast you'd panic if you felt it move.
You don't. Your feet are rooted, here.
Move them. See landscapes shift round you.

Speak. You'll make things come, and go.
It's easy: *The grass. The firework-burst.*
Think of a colour, any colour but red.
Instantly visualise: *lipgloss. Blood.*

Read: *'storms that scythe off rooftops*
start with the twitch of a butterfly's wings'.
Tape talk shows, game shows. *News At Ten.*
Rewind them. Watch them again. Again.

Know language means nothing, in itself.
Signified, sign. It's arbitrary.
What you say is conditioned by habit, power:
The water's dark. The cat's on fire.

Blackbirds are dinosaurs. This is true.
Evolution. There's fossil proof.
They strut the earth as if they own it still,
croak feebly, mock you. Live on worms.

Take all this too literally, personally.
Mix in the contents of one day's news.
Leave to stand in the way you live.
Think deeply, continually. Fall in love.

Then eliminate prejudice, defences, lies.
Take a concept like Justice. The ABC.
Read history. Let the contrasts brew.
Take a walk, look around. And think it through.

Stanzas for the Harp

(after hen benillion, Welsh, c.1700 – 1800)

(i)

The garden yours, you choose
nettle-leaves, blackthorn flowers,
stand them in water
in a crystal vase
by a wall full of shadows
and streaks of light;
spurn what you call
the vulgar rose, the lilies'
melodramatic symbolism,
the scarlets, whites and indigos
of a thousand years'
standing, still going strong.
Rather, you say, take
the under-flowers, the untended,
uprooted, bonfired hordes;
keep faith with poison,
thorn and sting,
the poise of the dangerous
unyielding strains
that – once barred from Eden –
were wholly ours.

(ii)

That Sunday, the bell-ropes tied
just out of reach
you strained on tip-toe
to touch them. Would swing,
you said, like Tarzan

through the after-echo
of the noise you'd make.
But settled for an amplified
Fred Astaire, clicking
boot-heels on a parquet floor;
found the building
unpeturbed so sat and crossed,
uncrossed bare legs.
Swore later that *Christ in Judgement*
stared, His gaze averted,
turned Heavenward
when you caught His eye –
flushed with sunlight,
yet brightened, and satisfied.

(iii)

Words leave residues, cracks
in the throat, root-
filaments frail as the locks of hair
we once exchanged,
the vows we once came here to make
while the ocean swirled open
its huge, damp mouth
to swallow the sun. *Just so*,
you said, placed your mouth on mine,
the sky in tumult,
on the verge of rain
dramatic yet deferent
to gravity. *Just so*,
you say, now you walk alone
where wild thyme snaps concrete
paving slabs, salt wind
strips I-beams at the causeway's end
to a froth of rust
and you halt by a shrivelled

rosemary bush
to face an ocean, ironed featureless
as the sheets, undisturbed
on your hotel bed.

(iv)

My stumblings, *uhms*,
cross continents,
sweep in bit-streams
through time-zones, space.
Bounced off satellites
to your waiting ear
I inarticulate
what it was I'd meant:
I thought um you might
like umm… so
how's it, like I mean,
you know…
And you do know, somehow,
lower your voice,
pause briefly,
breathe echo, say:
yeah, missed you.

(v)

She is trailing lace, white silks
so pure they tarnish flesh,
keeps dangling keys on a loop at her waist,
a cardboard child
for fertility. She holds a bouquet
of meat-red roses close
to the waterfall that conceals a face
no longer hers.
When that veil lifts, her abdomen

draws crimson light
through embroidered flowers,
her dress re-woven
with capillaries –
then she hears, in the space
between granite walls,
between *solemn vows* and exchange of rings,
an echo sustained
like an organ note
among the timbers creaking in a cradled roof –
the cry of a cousin
or in-law's child that will not settle
or be silenced, quite.

(vi)

Two loaves, a pound of fish, kerosene
and tea. You begrudge the cost,
plough through slush to reach home, dry off,
drink hot milk laced with Scotch
and slowly feel your own flesh
thaw. Where you walk, your footprints,
pressed clean into snow, submit to erasure
in aquarium light. Like a ghost
you leave no trace of weight, disappearing,
soluble in this last conceit.
You await your chance to reply to this
with interest.

Transference

You take a seat in the yard
that shadows can't reach, your hair
a roost for all the light
the sun has spare. Dust-motes, particles
swarm and flare. Footballs
thump drily on the whitewashed walls
and lawnmower-hum, the dead-
afternoon, extravagant heat
of a time when – I can just recall –
my past excludes your kiss,
your nakedness, by only hours…
All desire, I aspire to trust,
your interest; you are thinking
of something – someone –
else. And because you are not
what I say you are
but wholly, irreducibly *just yourself*,
there is only the waiting,
the pitch-and-toss, the three-
card brag and ambiguity
of the human heart as it moves from stasis
to the brink of change. Prised open,
slowly, like a sliding door
or flower-head – unpeeling, drenched
in a bar of light – it dithers,
beats, sits warm in its cage.
Pauses. Then reciprocates.

Marginalia

Trees unravel at the edge of this field
like estuaries, arteries,
tentacles lifting the moon to its hook,
clear of the *borealis*
headlamps make. Your footprints in snowfall
trail over the marsh,
leave shoes of black water
exposed on the dark –
their negatives fix in your shallow heels
as the heavens move.
We sway, light-headed with monoxide fumes
and brandy flasks, feel
the earth tilt like a silver tray
on a turtle's back, the sky
like a colander too big for the hills,
metallic and rattling
as the whole thing spins. There's a wind,
all teeth and cavities
we both walk through
where the traces of your blood-warm voice
disperse on cold. We stumble
uphill with a day-glo violet sword
retrieved from a toybox,
knuckles whitening on each-other's arms,
our footsteps brittle,
unsynchronised… Despite present tense
it's the past, of course. *Us.*
But you hear, and answer: *that's not how it was.*
Maybe, once, with someone else?
Your eyelids fit like doors
in their frames – close, chase words
to a distant source.

The Bubble

(after Richard Crashaw, Bulla, c.1646)

Life is short. You come of age,
shake out curves of tender flesh
and stand, defined, at the water's edge.
When Venus stepped
from the rose-pink lip
of her open shell, walked on foam
and stopped the light
for the beat of a heart,
even she, seeing you,
would be speechless now.
You are dazzling, growing unseizable
as you swell to a world,
as you swoop and whirl
and hesitate, unfix the air
taking no one path.
You are veined, a glistening intoxicant,
a cloud that scatters
and rushes space,
a chaos that pursues itself
in all directions. If you pause, look down –
see the rivers flow
like blood in veins or light through blood,
slippery where sensations fuse
under wind and sun.
There's a blaze of jewels,
a deluge of flowers,
each flower a star in a grounded sky.
And now you are hovering
on the harvest light,
your body poured through an abundance
bright with all colours

as all colours merge
and torches fade. Here is the vein
of a delicate wave
stitching purple
through a wound of red;
here are the rivers, bright as milk
washing blood from the sea,
the corn-fields splashing their yellow hair
in a deep blue sky.
Where wild roses open, lilies freeze,
frosting scarlet,
blushed in turn
as roses set the frost on fire
and frosts extinguish the roses' flames.
All is surface, red tinged green,
green tinted red,
all white impure
and impurity cleansed
as your bubble rises, brief as life –
a comet or a Catherine Wheel
that however the edge of its starry tail
might glide and spark
will end in an orbit all its own.

from *The Protein Songs* (2005)

The Protein Songs

> "In science, as in the rest of life, the paths are paths only in retrospect…in the tree of life itself there seems to be play in the system: what look like swerves and random branches."
> – Jonathan Weiner: *Time, Love, Memory* (1999)

(i)

In the word is a beginning,
a fragmented alphabet,
a dish of peas or bottled flies,
a tray of printer's metal type,
a John Bull rubber-stamping kit
with half the letters missing
and no full-stops:

agctcgctga, gacttcctgg…

Now a single silver disc
whirrs, unreels
three billion chemical base pairs,
a scroll of letters, *a-c-t-g*,
expansive as the biosphere,
its flows and anagrams, chants and drones,
unravelling the names of Sumerian gods
in the electronic bowl
of a laptop-drive –

agctcgctga, gacttcctgg…

like an overture.

(ii)

Here are the song-line's component notes,
scrawled in the margins
of a petrie dish
where phage is eaten by viruses,
spores proliferate, fruit-flies swarm,
fungi, mould and nematodes
spread through moisture, cultures,
ascending orders and taxonomies;

Eukaryota,
        Metazoa,
                Chordata…

links the wave of frogs that surges up
from tidal pools
with the storm of locusts, the shoal of fish,
the handful of wheat-seed
with the nest of ants,
the bramble, dragonfly, onion, owl;
joins beetle to blue whale,
lizard to cormorant and spider's web:
in toads and water
and *Phycomyces* we trace our names.

(iii)

There are songs in the darkness,
voices, harmonies, rounds.
There are moon and stars and candlelight
where women in night-gowns
gathered around an open tent
find unison as the warm night air
drifts in from the sea
and twelve voices climb an ascending scale:

Craniata,
        Vertebrata,
                Euteleostomi...

The notes – A, G, C –
rearrange like genes in a chromosome
change the shape
of the melody with every breath
to a different song,
the breath itself to random words.
The human voice, singing to and of itself
as it evolved itself to do:

Mammalia,
        Eutheria,
                Primate...

(iv)

But what evolves? The kora player in next-door's yard,
tickling rivers from strings and a hollow gourd,
breaks the heart more easily when the dusk sets in
than the multi-tracked choir inside the CD machine.

(v)

Still, the heart recovers, cell by cell,
and the heat of the sun, now stored in her naked back,
abandons itself to the stasis and pulse
of cicadas, fire-flies and insect-wings
in the air outside. Grapes hang, molecular, on twisted vines.
Each unripe sphere ascends its stalk
on a programmed course:

Catarrhini,
        Hominidae,
                Homo.

We reach our end in breathing,
in protein songs that spill into flesh,
the miniscule shoals of fish
that run their patterns
just below the waves
like code in a laptop, a compound in blood.

(vi)

What we remember, faintly,
in this deep blue hour
far from beginnings – the world's, and ours -
is how to open, turn, recall ourselves
up to our ribs in a crystal sea
where shredded ribbons of seaweed
like audiotape
form vast, dark slicks
and the evidence of three billion years
washes in on the tide.

(vii)

And now the winds return -
the genome's *Torah* is chanted plain
as a choir of scholars in a thousand labs worldwide
programme machinery to extract one word
from all creation,
the lines of a ragged, unsettling song:

agctcgctga, gacttcctgg…

What we have been is now written.
What we become remains blank.

That Afternoon

She sleeps, and into consciousness
swim fish and flatworms, a cloud of moths;
termites building ziggurats, beetles crossing tarmac roads.

She turns, and from the midday heat
comes a fever of lizards with iridescent crests,
a carpet of serpents, a sunlit rain of frogs.

She murmurs, and as her body twists
trilobites scurry through some offshore reef,
jellyfish ripple translucently with the flow of the mind.

She stretches, her leg muscles flexing
like the wings of a ray in the turbulence,
prised from sand to pulse and float like breathing gills

on the lip of the beach. When she wakes,
beside her on these floral sheets is a body, of the species *hominid*,
picking crumbs from the folds of its clothes

like a chimp with a straw at a termite-nest.
In the window, the windows of another house,
red brick and rain, the aquatic light of TV in a darkened room.

Siesta Hour

(i)

A monastery of scientists in the gathering light
peer through tiny windows at the refined machine

of a fruit-fly no bigger than this comma, here,
its multiplicity of precision-tooled parts,

its knowledge, memory, sense of time and love
becoming a world in miniature, not unlike our own.

(ii)

On a bed, elsewhere, pale bodies entwine,
arm around shoulder, thigh pressed to calf,

ankle to kneecap, wrist circling rib… We sleep,
our body-clocks set by DNA, our tangle of joints,

our flesh and sweat, our skins encoded in strings and pairs.
Here are chromosomes, proteins, breath and bone,

the white crystal lattice of *drosophilia's* eye
stirring connections with Mendel's peas,

the handfuls of grass seed that carry downwind
to flourish in hedgerows miles away – the legs

of this insect, weighted with pollen globes,
that touch down, briefly, on her abdomen,

gently dust her sweat with fertile gold. All connects,
the seed to the bird to the fox to the ground.

In this midday heat that unravels all sense
the mind plays roulette with random words:

…*half-blind, vermilion, white & brown,
cinnabar, fruitless, foraging, forked*…

The sun pours warmth through empty glass,
casts a glow around limbs, laces shadows through hair,

makes star-fields of dust and blown dandelion seed,
conjures rainbows from bottles and whitewashed walls.

(iii)

Light gleams on the snow of spores and seeds
that drift in brightness, seeking open flowers.

There's a song in the leaves of the poplar trees
as they turn and shimmer, as the earth revolves

and their roots adjust. I clench my toes in my sandals
when they slip as I walk, see shadows shrinking

as the sun ascends. The hedgerow roses and geraniums
gape and wilt in the heat, flushed with colour,

pheromones, pollens, scents. All will melt in siesta hour
to soft, moist flesh and flows of blood, to thirst,

the thought that connects a look to a touch,
a cellular yearning that floods the brain

with these bodies – air with salt water, fire and earth.
The vulva and labia in their nest of hair

might be a fruit fly's mandible, an oyster's tongue,
a gill or orchid or opened ripening fruit

for this toadstool, sea slug, broken dandelion stalk
leaking milk white fluid that I bear in my hand.

from *Emblems* (2009)

A Trick Of The Light

> "See how these fruitful kernels, being cast
>   Upon the earth, how thick they spring!"
> – Francis Quarles: *Emblems II/Epigram* (1635)

Walking at night, we catch ourselves on CCTV
behind the plate glass doors of the department store,
glance up through bikinis and sun-tan oils
to face the lens. *Escape To Paradise*
say the open skies and crystal seas
of St Lucia, Barbados or wherever it is
as they glaze the queue for the 279
to Tottenham and Waltham Cross
with coloured light. Underfoot, the litter of *Perfect Skin,
Live To The Max* and *Fun, Fun, Fun*
swirl on a cyclone of freezing wind
like tumbleweed in a frontier town.
Overhead, on billboards flashed bright with floods
and florescent strips, the smiling, quietly
confident face of the woman who knows
her needs are met, the man whose
chiselled, sun-warmed limbs
frame a six-pack of airbrushed skin.
Steel shutters and notices – *Group 4 Patrol* –
detach these pleasures from our ownership.
The newsagent's shelves of plaster Saints
and Sacred Hearts sleep among signs
for *The Sun* and *Mars*. We count out change,
move our weight from foot to aching foot.
We are going home on whichever bus comes first.

Slapstick (Coda)

"...true emblems of sweetness, these bees do bring
  Honey in their mouths, in their tails a sting."
— Francis Quarles: *Emblems III/Epigram* (1635)

Here is the summer's final sting, subs and baguettes
in a sandwich bar, insects strewn on the window sills

after repeatedly drumming glass and steam
to reach the air. Here is a handful of herring gulls,

a tourist's sandal lost to the wind, a gutter
where sand and rainwater flood double yellows and parking bays.

On the harbour's Silurian mudstone walls, a glitter of mica,
fossil moss, the moonlight shadows of deserted boats.

They nod, abstracted, perform gamelan rites
for the sound alone – garlands of litter festoon rising tides,

sing *Bali Hai* as cold bells chime. Fibreglass floats tap
wooden ribs and keels, echo in the spaces where winter fell

and something ended, three generations back. Here
is the hollow, where a pavement drops to meet the beach

and wind carves its shelter in shale and flint.
A dog is barking. Car doors slam where headlamps shine

and a breeze turns, while the ocean casts its speckled stones
on the slate grey beach, as though reading runes.

Lichens, white jellyfish and bladder-wrack
fruit like vines in a forest at the end of the world.

The Archway Altarpiece

"All is vanity and vexation of spirit."
— *Ecclesiastes II:17*

Shit happens, he shrugs, then turns from his mate
to head for wherever he's going next,
draws thin denim round his shoulderblades
then shouts from the backboard as the bus pulls out,
forget it, y'hear me? There's nowt y'can do...
His voice fades fifty feet away to a trail of words
only the conductor and the angels hear
though he stands, his hand on the silver bar
till he's out of sight. *Still,* says the one he's left behind
to himself and the world, *still and all,*
kicking his heels as he lopes uphill with all the time
on the clock to spare. They're both sixteen.
I lean over railings, half a cigarette burning down
to the knuckle of my one free hand;
braced in the other between palm and thumb
is a yellow hardback *Satyricon*.
At my back, the dark, exhaust-stained stone
of *The Archway Clinic of Sexual Health*
extends asylum behind electric doors
to every conceivable shade of love.
In the subway, scrawled on a convex mirror,
Sexi Girls floats over pregnant steps,
Jason is Gay x 500 Times and *Im The KING*
like the outstretched arms of a crucifix
tagged in marker on either side.
I am waiting, expecting nothing in exchange for my time
but a smoke, Trimalchio, and the test's return.

Side-Effects

> "...wake now or never,
> For if thou nodd'st thou fall'st, and falling, fall forever."
> – Francis Quarles: *Emblems VII* (1635)

That morning you were lying-in, stirring sometimes
in the turbulence of an overcast, late-April heat,
dreaming of entering a pharmacy, drinking a cup of methadone
then rocking a lion to sleep in your arms
while stroking its mane in an olive grove.
It's the anti-depressants, you start to explain that night,
they leave me so lethargic I can barely move...
You are weighing Serge Gainsbourg and Brigitte Bardot
against Stereolab's *Refried Ectoplasm*,
Bonnie & Clyde against *Harmonium*,
seeking something, anything, that might lift the mood.
It's so hard, you say, *to want to be awake*
when there's only work, this room and debt to be conscious in...
You press POWER and PLAY, then set REPEAT.
I'm all right, really, just a bit run down.
Tell me a story. Keep me entertained.
There's a joke about penguins you've heard before,
a 'twenties cocktail called an '*Angel's Tit*'.
You turn away, stare out over rooftops, yards, yet listen hard,
follow the thoughts that slip unvoiced
behind the words I use. *It was strictly two-thirds cherry liqueur,*
one-third cream with a cherry on top.
You'd drink it and think you'd seen the face of God.
Buttercups nod on a darkening lawn
and ivy slumps like a safety-net
in the shadows thrown by a carriage-lamp.
You tell me you're watching your own mind work from a long way off,
does that make sense, or are you going mad?
The orange upglare of the skyline burns
like rushlight on armoured, unmoving clouds.

Underground

"My soul, sit thou a patient looker-on;
Judge not the play before the play is done…"
– Francis Quarles: *Emblems XV/Epigram* (1635)

The tube is hurtling through the dark, windows lacquered like a Chinese box
where faces, pale as breath condensed on glass, gaze through themselves
at the line of ghosts in a parallel train, nothing there but the heat and noise
of fetid tunnels veiled in black, the clatter of wheels on burnished rails,
thin pages turning as someone leaves through a sheaf of notes.
A woman who boarded two stops back is mumbling apocalypse from an
open book,
whispering hymns that barely shape her breath as she stares at her shoes:

All worldly things shall return to dust,
and we shall rise up to be judged –
we shall be clothed in naught but sin,
and His wrath shall pour like rain…

A man who clutches a child to his breast, its small mouth staining an aureole
in the powder-blue fleece of his tracksuit-top, glances uneasily right and left.
Yet we flow through the earth like words in a wire, the blood in a vein,
shall rise among gleaming escalators into the sunlight of the ticket halls.
We will flood junctions, stations, buildings, streets, like a power surge in
the circuitry
before a system crash. This is only a moment, a single forward step in time
that might have ended up anywhere, but seems to end right here.

from *The Apple Sequence* (2011)

The Apple Prologue

The apple is promiscuous, neither knows its place
nor accepts the limits of what it is.

The apple continually shifts its shape
until grafted by greenwood to a grounded root.

The apple spreads from garden to field,
from deciduous copse to commercial farm.

The apple mutates, from seed inside the sweetest fruit
to giant sour globe or golf-ball crab.

The apple is heterogeneous, open to change:
its gene-codes run viral in orchard and hedge.

The apple was born in China and Kazakhstan,
where *Malus sieversii* first emerged from the wild.

The apple gave birth to original sin,
one bite of its flesh bringing shame to skin.

The apple is a relative of the briar rose,
barely recognisable once the blossom fades.

The apple alights like an insect swarm
in hedgerows when orchards are grubbed and gone.

The apple's graft rootstock and knife-cut wood
might be strangers till the wound is healed.

Apple seeds might flourish by a motorway's side,
in new varieties, sweeter than any known before.

For the apple will spread from garden to field,
from deciduous copse to commercial farm.

The apple will continually shift its shape
until grafted by greenwood to a grounded root.

And the apple is promiscuous: neither knows its place
nor accepts the limits of what it is.

The Apple Migrations

"Apples are known to have been gathered in the Neolithic and Bronze Age in the Near East and Europe, and all archaeological findings indicate a fruit size compatible with those of the wild *M. sylvestris*, a species bearing small astringent and acidulate fruits. Sweet apples corresponding to extant domestic apples appeared in the Near East around 4,000 years ago, at the time when the grafting technology used to propagate the highly heterozygous and self-incompatible apple was becoming available. From the Middle East, the apple passed to the Greeks and Romans, who spread fruit cultivation across Europe…"
– Riccardo Velasco et al: *The genome of the domesticated apple (Nature Genetics,* vol.42, 2010*)*

(i)

To England from алма, apple-city of Kazakhstan
from forest and hedgerow to garden tree:

by way of Roman road and dropped brown seed,
by basket and pack-mule to Hereford field;

from mountain and garden to lush Kent hill,
Thames-side parkland to Essex wood.

(ii)

To England from 新疆, in Chinese Turkestan,
from white rose-blossom to blushed green fruit;

from wild apple forest to table stained with wine,
from *the egg to the apples* at a garden feast.

This is where discarded pips strike fresh roots
from fallen cores among grass-softened stones.

(iii)

To England from غات ىرلګهت, a jagged mountain
where snow meets cloud within sight of Gods;

a celestial, serrated ridge of stone that shows from space,
a surging wave where China touches Kyrgyzstan.

(iv)

To England from the armies of Μακεδονίας
where sweet dwarf apples eaten by Alexander's men,

once pulled from the earth of Kazakhstan,
are carried back from battle to town and home,

cast out into gardens, among beds of rain and sun,
build root-stocks resistant to drought and frost.

(v)

To England from Almaty's domed mosques
where business towers of blue steel and glass

shadow open roads, surrounding hills and plains.
Oceans of rose-leaf and wild apple-flowers

forge seeds to be lifted on a Kazakh breeze
then dropped, brought west by birds and fertilized.

Cold soils adopt them: hand-knives graft their wood.
New fruits grow from the changing root.

(vi)

In England, from orchard to monger of *Costard* fruit
among open drains in London, York and Wells,

from Lowland walled-garden to city street at Lent,
Lincoln graveyard to earth in a Southwell pot,

from warm Kent orangery to East Malling's fields,
abandoned monastery to enclosed corn-maze,

in wind and mist where gardens erode from cliffs,
the apple roots, bears apples, again mutates.

(vii)

From England, apples cross the globe and hybridize,
trace lines of empire, trade, territories held or lost

on a long migration whose tangled paths appear
like routes sketched out on giant airport maps:

apples weave a net of wood round the globe, advance
one root-tip, one leaf-stem, one seed at a time.

Notes:

Алма (Alma, meaning apple: a city noted for apple production in Kazakhstan)

新疆 (Xinjiang, autonomous region of North East China)

تەڭرى تاغ (Uyghur script for the Chinese 天山, *Tian Shan*, or Celestial Mountain)

Μακεδονίας (Macedon, ancient Greek kingdom of Alexander the Great)

Costard (Culinary apple variety, introduced to England in the early Middle Ages)

The Roots of the Apple

(i) *East Malling, 1912*

These roots are hung on air,
nets of wood
strung like a skirt
held open for courtesying
against a white sheet;

so we measure their spread,
the true extent
of their miraculous work
among mole-tunnels,
pot shards and rich clay soils;

we observe how each hair,
each finger-thick
root and stub,
every node and growing stem
in this nervous system

of exposed root draws breath
from grains of earth,
absorbs moisture,
pushes frail tips
through the hard ground,

fuels a heavy trunk and bough
then delivers fruit.
Daily we notch
new growth in chalk,
log each fractional

forward move of plant-cell and sap
where its tendrils swim
through soil
like worms or eels,
regenerating lizards' tails,

live as our camera's electric light
in these cellars,
corridors,
observation rooms
we shiver in while roots unfurl.

(ii) *Herefordshire, 2011*

A stand of trees aligned to the horizon,
a vast peach moon sliced by a knife of grass
where orchards are drilled
in battalion lines,
green circuits hardwired to earth,
each one a standard height and form.

What is known is their girth and spread,
their nutrient demands, size of leaf,
susceptibility to blight,
their yield of fruit;
what were once the wildings
of field and hedge are standardized here

to mirror, endlessly, one another's shapes
in fields laid for productivity
where *Braeburn*
and *Cox's Orange Pippin* thrive,
balance acids and sugars, consistent as clones,
wrap spherical pulps in identical skins.

Egremont Russet

from: *The Naming of Apples (Thirteen Varieties)*

I am remembering now, for no better reason
than that it is in my mind – like a letter
retrieved from attic junk, an object surfacing
in a clogged canal – that photograph found five years ago,
a marker lost between chapters three and four
of *The Apple Book,* where *Egremont Russet*
meets *Ellison's Orange* and *Epicure*:
an image of a girl in a pale green dress, a silk scarf
patterned with apple-halves
flung off one shoulder, a bough in a storm,
where she stands, half a century back, in bleached-out tones,
her ladder propped among apple leaves,
a woven basket and dead weight of Russets cupped
like the pendulum of a grandfather clock
on the crook of her arm. That ladder sways,
the clouds too close, and all seems precarious,
from the Kodachrome colours in that fading print
to the ground itself, studded with trees
that would soon be grubbed-up, cast aside,
leaving this trace of sunlight, apples and a girl behind.

James Grieve

from: *The Naming of Apples (Thirteen Varieties)*

This is finance, a ploughed field
showing blooms of ochre earth
sliced through with black,
a flood-lake glistening, abandoned caravan,
a woodpile and a heap of scrap:
this is an exit strategy, in its final phase.

Blossoming among the brewery towers,
waterlogged in a heavy soil,
a stand of magnolia and apple trees,
steels rusting on a siding's walls
where lichen marks a boundary line
between brownfield and railway,

weed and flower. It is already September,
summer barely settled in,
yet apples grow so abundantly
these branches strain. This is finance,
proliferation breeding mass,
inaccessible harvests in parched seed-grass.

Hidden Rose

from: *The Naming of Apples (Thirteen Varieties)*

Cut open, the inner flesh is pink as nail-polish,
a tissue's lipstick kiss, diluted elderberry in a muslin weave.
Its smooth texture carries a sweet, tart kick.
There's no trace of red in the wood or leaves
and fruit are short-lived on the tree when ripe.
It's as though pomegranites, enchanted into apple-hood,
froze as they changed on first sight of blood.

Newton's Wonder

from: *The Naming of Apples (Thirteen Varieties)*

A winding track between a pair of rocks,
white smoke exhaled from cooling towers
beside the River Soar – all floats over
like apple blossom drifting in a reflected sky.

The pinched faces in Leonardo's clouds,
mountains conjured from lichen-bloomed walls,
frowsy with mosses and dry cement,
play on the mind when night descends

and shadows lengthen like apple boughs
in growing times. Are things really any worse
with the world? A day might slide inexorably
into freezing dark between sun and dawn,

light sieve through threadbare cloud
like syrup poured over apples from a glistening tin.
Colours vanish, one by one, clothes unpegged
from washing-lines and taken in.

No progression is ever clear or permanent:
among these girders, collapsing walls
where windfalls scatter at the foot of a tree
and a hubcap makes a grounded moon

night amplifies, echoes on the coming frost.
I brush apple-skins with my own white breath.
Newton's Wonder considers and tests
the gravity drawing all its ripest fruit to earth.

The Apple's Song in Autumn

Let the blossom tarnish, the paired globes
of the ripening fruit be rich with juice.

Let the meeting of pulp and slab of wood
press cider that washes away ourselves,

fills the cup, lets the glass mug drain
as leaves grant cover for the drunken maid

and the boy whose sheep are gone astray
before the first blast of winter

brings them all, shivering, back to him.
Then we'll know the autumn's done.

Till then, let's stay in the apple-shade
where sun's still warm and warm rain falls

to stroke our skins. Let us press graft-wood
to the moist split in the apple's trunk,

let green lichen flourish, the long knot
in dark wood be lips parted for a first kiss.

Let thick moss gather like a maiden's beard
where grained boughs part like spread thighs

to slow the coming of winter's chill.
Let the moon stay yellow, our flesh weak.

Let apple juice flow by the jug from trees.
Christ, keep us from chapel till first frosts strike.

Things That Are Not Apples

"A stone from the hand of a friend is an apple."
– Proverb, origin unknown.

Things that are not apples might include
this wax fruit piled in a white bowl,
a jade pebble polished or blushed with red,
an apple carved from apple wood
to scent a room. Might include
roses (though the leaves and blossom
are much alike), gall apples that incubate
larval wasps in boles of bark
on the new-grown twigs of summer oaks.
Might include cider, chutney, apple sauce,
cups of steaming hot apple juice,
though all those things *were* apples once.
Things that are not apples are iPads,
smart-phones, shiny tablets filled with lithium
and coltan chips; late Beatles records
and London shops; a plump child's cheeks
or a place in the eye. Things that are not apples
(even without white grubs at their hearts,
slugs on their skins) are metaphors
for sin and corrupted youth: summer lawns,
bedrooms and first-car back-seats
where kisses are stolen in symbolic ways
we've seen a dozen, a hundred, times before,
each saying: *this is the end of love.*
Things that are not apples are quince,
pear, orange and peach, apricot
and pineapple. Things that are not apples
are the white pulp of a paper mill,
the skin of a fish, the dark tear-drop pip
of a cherry-stone and the leather

of a cricket ball; range from the egg of a bud
to a blossom's white frill, a marble sphere
to the blown glass of a fishing float.
These things are *not* apples, round or red,
leafed and stemmed as they seem.
Some taste of apple, carry apple-scents,
show off qualities we think of as *apple-like*
in their shapes and forms. But in the end,
like juices made of concentrate
or the inflated pulp and perfect skins
of packaged apples in supermarket aisles,
they're quick to fool the taste and glance
but are not (and will never be) apples, quite.

A Grubbed Orchard (Does Spring Come...?)

(after Yi Sang-hwa, Korean, 1900 – 1943)

Does spring come just the same to stolen fields
as to fields that remain in common hands?

Here, where this narrow path between fences climbs
toward a point where clouds and green grass touch,

I catch cool breezes on the back of my neck,
listen for the whispered names and breaths of leaves

that nudge me on though the going's hard.
A lark sings, like a young girl hiding behind a hedge,

and I know this ground, where apple trees heavy
with the night's long rain hold brambles tangled

like my lover's hair the moment before she wakes,
the moment I rise, dizzy, on the precipice of being still asleep,

stretch my limbs then stand, unsteady, upright.
I walk lightly, now. I can feel my shoulders picking up

some distant rhythm from across the fields
where wind shuffles the grass, sparse violets grow

and apples fall: and all at once I recall that girl
whose face I once noticed when she stooped and smiled,

picking weeds from a bed of flowers, apple blossoms
caught in the waterfall of her blue-black hair.

I wanted a scythe, then, a spade or rake in my hands,
to feel that soft ground yield beneath my feet,

to work the earth, feel my body run with sweat
as though I were showering in cascades of apple juice.

But these are only thoughts, restless as children
at play by the brook, going nowhere as I'm walking on,

breathing in the green scent of spring grass,
the verdant sorrow of knowing only this:

that behind barbed wire whole orchards burned.
Here are the stumps where those apples were.

I note these fields, once ours, blanked round in steel:
stolen by fences that turned the whole spring sour.

The Order of Seasons

"Essence of winter sleep is on the night,
the scent of apples: I am drowsing off…"
– Robert Frost: *After Apple Picking* (1915)

(i)

Deep November. The order of seasons shifts.
Japanese knotweed scythed from the ground,
is black stalks, open white hollow mouths,
tubeworms clustered on a mulched sea-bed of autumn brown.
It absorbs light, chokes these few frail shoots of green
holding on among the knotweed's roots
like fish in the weave of a tightening net.
And here are cigarette butts, paper cups, sheets of newsprint
blown to the lea of a railway arch, already slippery
as their slopes decay: their seditious move
against the picturesque is almost done.
Worms graze, woodlice tumble like trilobites
from age to age; pigeon, blackbird, the odd stray dog
or urban fox, dark bacterium, black meat-fly,
moss and mould-spore, all feed here, where waste ferments,
cold to the touch, brews its liquor of fertile mulch.
Come spring, or summer, when cold wet weather
gives way to warm, what were once *the seasons*
start to blur and fuse: are here, then gone.
Knotweed rises, new species of lichen, moss and mould
that bend with the weather like finches' beaks
and theologies. Only fern and woodlouse hold their form.
The apple stays constant through restlessness.

(ii)

The season deepens, gathers wind-blown leaves
from the apple tree by the garden gate:
winter prepares its assault of frost and rain.
The last of summer retreats to its root,
lies low in the earth as autumn's afternoons set in,
long enough to chill the lawn, so dark
your face reflects in a window's glass at noon.
Was there an instant, one November night,
when our time together outweighed our years apart?
Did the scales tilt slightly, the season turn,
when you glanced up, saw the sunlight writhe
in its quilt of cloud and, yawning, shine
as its thin light gathered on an apple bough,
with branches tangled in roses' strings?
Did it seem, in that instant, as though trunk and root
were kept upright by the roses' threads,
leaves that fluttered where honeysuckle drooped
over moss, like streamers at a party's end?
And if the storms and seasons, days and hours,
pass by us now, quick as clouds,
is there time left over to even half-attend
those orchards leaning like planks on the night,
drunk, as we are, on pressed pulp and juice?

(iii)

There is a labyrinth at the heart of bone,
the echo and tremor of waves in a shell
where tides withdraw through a white maze.
There is the star inside an apple core
taking imprints of weathered teeth,
a body in seed time that blossoms, fruits,
wakes when cider's sweet acid taste
stings the tongue and warms the throat.
There are photographs, negatives, phrases:
electronic traces that slowly fade.
There are orchards under the ribs and skin,
red fruit hung in chest and abdomen;
lung and liver, stomach, kidney, heart,
the apples left over when our seasons end
and heat recedes in the hollow bone
whose corals grow brittle in a net of veins.
What's left then but drink? We'll take inside us
this cold night air, lie back on grass
feel its chill on our bodies at 3am
beneath an apple moon, a nest of clouds.
Hot cider will pass from hand to hand,
its taste carry through every kiss.
This is citrus in an open wound,
apples flooding our bitten tongues
with the sting of flesh we only came to love
when all its powers began to fade.

Uncollected Poems (2006 – 2014)

Lines after Abbas Ibn Al-Ahnaf

(for Suzie)

Love plants its trees in the heart,
waters and tends their deepening roots,
calls new growth to begin again each spring.

All summer, birds will flock here to nest,
sing among the ripening fruits
each autumn presses to strong, sweet wine.

And today, your face is a winter moon,
an apple that a stubborn bough,
however the winds blow, will not let fall.

(750 – 809 AD)

The Blue Wolves and the Wheelbarrow

(i.m Eva Švankmajerová, 1940 – 2005)

"...a salute to a strange ritual/that is called life..."
– Eva Švankmajerová: *Chance*

and the blue wolves run from the ocean,
and the child has swallowed the wheelbarrow whole

On the wall is this canvas, like a window cut
from one world to another, with teeth between,

from late afternoon above autumnal Prague
to green ocean under livid yellow sun,

from cobbled streets where crumbling walls mark time
to blue wolves flying in frozen arcs,

flags empty as brassieres on the balconies of apartment-blocks,
ammonites, narwhal shells, knives and forks,

the moon above Černínská like a dinner-plate
sliced by clouds made by coffee-pots vibrating on stoves.

A mother, her dark mouth open and issuing storms,
sees her child ascend through a tablecloth,

eat hammer and sickle, eagle and stars and stripes,
eat wheelbarrows, pigs and horses whole.

and the blue wolves flee from the ocean,
and the child is chewing the wheelbarrow up

Raindrops make honey from vitrified stone,
white vulvas of lava open to speak in the cave.

Waters are thundering deep underground,
breathing like engines, coughing lungsful of flowers,

chambers of echoes whose capillaries flow
with language in a rising flood:

onto fog onto death and tender disappointments…
I only whisper, but there was a fire

It burns crimson, yellow, like an upended dress,
leaves a fur of embers to rake over, here,

eggshells, coals and the bones from meat
glowing black and orange, still giving heat.

and the blue wolves take flight from the ocean,
and the child is digesting the wheelbarrow now

Birch trees tremble in the autumn wood,
their fingernails grown out like twigs from hands.

What was dead becomes living: a sewing machine,
a beating heart wrapped in newspaper, cold…

Milk sweats like gelignite under pond-sheets of ice,
comes to the boil in a simmering pot on a stove

where grass runs to sand, pavements to clay.
Here is bread turned to flesh beneath human skin,

sackcloth inhaling a living shape, listening
through cold and rain for noises sounding beyond its walls:

girls skipping and rhyming and clicking ropes on the stones
of stairways and walls full of bullet-holes.

and the blue wolves get clear of the ocean,
and the child almost choked on the wheelbarrow, once

Echoes tap their mahogany ivory-tipped canes
on the cobbles outside Michalská's *Sex Machines Museum*,

hypnotised by mannequins that squat astride
spinning wheels of perished rubber tongues,

truncheons heavy as dildoes in the hands of police,
a feathered arm dextrous as an elephant's trunk in a circus act.

Money jangles, yearning for metal slots
to warm with pheromones beneath the pads of thumbs

lift gooseflesh on wood and fibreglass,
set nerves trembling in arms, and in under-arms...

Movies are flickering on the falling rain,
cast shadows of breasts, pale blue skins and body-hair

through galaxies of luminous, anxious dust.
Our currencies harden, turn flaccid, melt,

flow uphill and gather behind Loreto's ornate façade
where Saints and turrets and turning marble stairs

seem garish as a fairground organ-case. Monkeys dance:
a bell chimes in a music box, and minds are lost.

and the blue wolves run from the ocean,
and the child has swallowed the wheelbarrow whole

Black Glass

(i.m. Douglas Houston, 1947 – 2013)

"Each new development in cinema might, paradoxically, be taking the medium closer to its origins: in fact, it may be the case that cinema has not yet been invented…"
– Andre Bazin: *The Myth of Total Cinema* (1946)

(i)

Images consume us when they embrace the eye:
a white star in the hook of the moon,
an empty tower block with one burnt floor,
the red sun winching slowly down,
thinning out across a violet sky.
A woodland is garnished with milk-weak light,
there is glass on a pebble, a lens in mud.
Look again at these images the eye absorbs:
grains in a sugar bowl on a linen cloth,
liquid sugar dissolving a fractured tooth.

(ii)

This is the current that floods a convex lens,
a signal trembling in the optic nerve,
the familiar blue-tinged flare and fade
that jumps each synapse it comes across
with a jolt and shudder, some remembered sight –
the twine of smoke from an incense stick,
a carpet patterned in paisley swirls.
This is memory: light leaping a deep crevasse.
This is shadow etched in a skin of glass
whose edges soften as the world's erased.

(iii)

A cold fire burns in every house we pass.
In every room where a hearth might be,
plasma screens and cathode tubes
glow ocean-blue, cast the light of coral
and turning shoals on a glass decanter, picture frame,
the dark brass bracket of a fire-surround.
The wrong news gathers like dust on a shelf,
as shells pierce the whitewashed walls of homes,
explode the sides of open trucks
in far-off deserts and poppy fields.

(iv)

The world outside is consumed entire:
what escapes the flames does not exist.
Here is the scrolling infinity sign
of a film reel passing through strobes of light,
movement conjured, blink by blink,
from the loop of a ribbon, clatter of wheels,
a flicker of shutters, a shadowed screen.
The image shifts: *forests steeped in silver light,*
grains in a sugar bowl on a linen cloth,
one star hanging on the moon's white hook.

(v)

The image fades or begins to change,
the posture shifts by a fraction
to left or right; the greenhouse is flooded
with shade or sun. One hand's raised,
a finger cocked, one plunged in a pocket
to turn a coin that will soon be spent.
Some store consciousness in pockets, tins,
etch it on glass and pasteboard cards.
What is stored in attics and garden sheds
is what recalls us when all else fails.

(vi)

The gap between traces and what they show
might be close as particles, cells or stars,
intimate as mountains on that TV screen
glimpsed in a neighbour's window
when the war is long past its seventh year.
Let what remains of all this not be editorials
and commercial reels, but images,
caught just in the instant they embraced the eye:
a cluster of rooftops not seen for years,
a vanished street that burns with shade.

Zeropolis, or Shelley in Las Vegas

"The sense of day and night, of false and true/Was dead within me..."
– Shelley: *The Revolt of Islam, Canto III, Stanza XXIV* (1818)

(i)

So now we come into the wide main street, the summer ended,
the sun bright on every concrete wall, neon sleeping
in its aluminium frames. Mary, you would not know Las Vegas
by its daylight face, by the humming traffic on Fremont Street,
the suits that pass each glazed façade, check themselves,
holding phones to ears in depthless ponds of shaded dark.
They move from office block to scarlet burger hall,
from mall to underworld motel, each in pursuit of a losing streak
he can call his own and hold to his heart. All vision is lost,
dissolved in the desert's white-crowned sun at noon.

(ii)

I'll go on. It will be dark again soon enough, that fallen light
drawing the city out from beneath the stone of its daylight sleep.
The land is parched in every part, yet this city draws water
from pipes in the earth, sprays all through fountains
and false canals as Venice partners the pyramids
and Florence collides with London Bridge on a shopping mall.
Time distends. Light's faked so seasons and weeks
neither move nor change. I might grow old here in a single day,
totter on sticks from machine to table to ice-cream bar,
a calf being fattened, bled white, emptied out in sacrifice.

(iii)

Under gleaming strip-lights lines of men turn grey, feed coins
to the mouths of bright machines: silver, gold.
All's consumed alike with a hollow flicker and dance of light,
a chime of bells. Once an hour one machine in ten
might clatter and flash like a summer storm, belch treasure
from its cog-wheel guts into the plastic bucket held by the blessed.
Then all will quieten to a lurid calm, the suckling reflection
of that same pale face in the hypnotic strobe of a scrying-glass:
the kind a storybook Witch might use to cast a curse –
a curse like this, or worse, on one who'd done her wrong.

(iv)

Mary, you will think this strange, but I tell you I saw with my
                                                    own dry eyes
a woman weeping upon a slot machine, a farmhand pouring
golden coins into a velvet trough as though emptying slops
for a sty of pigs. A man might spin his house on a wheel
and, feeling nothing but the passing spur of a split-second quirk
of gravity, throw his spirit after it on the turn of a card.
Mary, this is how things are. This is the city that spread its ways
through all the capitals and financial halls of the world.
A billion ghosts count coins, pull levers among mirrors and lights.
Beyond, a desert, where shadows deepen unglimpsed outside.

Instructions for Baking the Nottingham Golem

Gather sugar crystals, a pinch of salt,
two broken eggs in a glass bowl,
white flour ground fine as porcelain,
flood-water scooped from any bend in the Trent
where the moon shines as reflected light.

Decant this water one cup at a time
all the while intoning lines
from your chosen alchemical chant or prayer.
Blend in a basin fired from flesh-pink clay:
add spit, blood, hair and a pinch of ash.

Shape this matter by stroke and touch.
Work your fingers as though immersed in sex,
firm but circling in the slippery mix
that slowly ripens to the colour of skin
as limbs and trunk find human form.

Keep kneading, palm by thumb
by finger-tip, heel of hand by roll of wrist,
until what takes shape is firm enough to stand.
Add the final details: etch in tendons,
finger-nails, eyelids, lashes, lips.

Wet a sable brush in a spoon of milk,
paint the skin and cover with a dampened cloth.
Leave undisturbed to prove, then wait.
You may now find yourself with an urge to bathe,
feel your skin grown sensitive,

slide one warm hand over torso, thighs,
press gentle fingers into pubic hair.
Do not resist. Let that slow unraveling ache
be soothed, your muscles tense
and flesh swell: let those pressures build

till the whole house jumps. Only then
might this form draw breath,
a sudden gasp beneath the cloth
that possesses you. Only now should you return
to lift that milk-scented linen shroud.

Do not stop. This thing you've made is yours.
You may observe a cold trace of breath,
flour-dust hanging in the air,
a small twitch inside an ashen wrist. Show no fear.
Gather your stones. Prepare the fire.

A Simultaneous Translation (April 10, 2013)

A Simultaneous Translation is made up of texts derived from a Korean Central News Agency (KCNA) press release dated December 17, 2011, documenting the "strange natural phenomena" it claimed were neutrally witnessed in North Korea at the time of Kim Jong-il's death. This source text was manipulated in response to the comparable atmosphere of propaganda created by the build-up to Margaret Thatcher's quasi-state funeral in April 2013.

(i)

Today we stand in the glow of cleansing propaganda
while peculiar natural wonders are observed
on Mt. Paektu, Jong Il Peak
and Tonghung Hill in Hamhung City,
in the transparent glare of white light shining
from the stones of Parliament Square and Westminster.

(ii)

Today, we hear of a Parliament recalled
at some great and unexplained expense to citizens
so that memory might be trussed for sacrifice
at the feet of Our Leader's statue
on a day when all the people are mourning
the continuance of Our Leader's work
in bitterest sorrow.

(iii)

On the morning of April 10
layers of ice were broken on Lake Chon on Mt. Paektu,
on the Serpentine in St James's Park,
among the roses behind Temple Bar.
The lake, the city, the water,
all shook with big noise.
The cameras did not draw back from the edge
but continued turning.

(iv)

The Group for Comprehensive Exploration
of Lake Chon on Mt. Paektu
and The Group for Comprehensive Maintenance
of St James's Park,
both announced it was the first time
such a big noise was heard
from the ridge of Janggun Peak and the lake,
from the junction between Whitehall and Trafalgar Square.
All the exposed film in our cameras turned white.

(v)

The temperature on Mt. Paektu
and around the trees of St James's Park that day
registered 22.4 degrees Centigrade below Zero.
There was strong wind
accompanied by a snowstorm
which travelled through the atmosphere
at a speed of 18 metres per second.
All this was measured by Our Leader's research staff.

(vi)

The snowstorm stopped blowing
all of a sudden
from the dawn of Tuesday
and heavy clouds
were seen hanging around Hyangdo Peak
and above the River Thames.

(vii)

At 8:05am the sky began turning red
with sunrise on the horizon.
The peaks of the waves on the River Thames
and Hyangdo Mountain
looked like pictures, wide and glowing.

(viii)

Our Leader's autographic writings
speak of a "Steadfast Doctrine to the West and North"
as the Manchurian crane might fly
in a solitary, undeviating straight line
above "Mt. Paektu, Holy Mountain of Revolution"
to alight months later
on one span of Westminster Bridge.

(ix)

"When a Great Leader is taken from our midst
we must bow our heads in gratitude
set all remembrance of deeds aside.
We must accept the justice of that Leader's rule:
only then is proper respect shown
and Our Leader's Greatness made Our Truth."

(x)

The stones around us glow brightly.
This phenomenon lasts until 5am.

(xi)

This glow in the stones at 5am was seen atop Jong Il Peak
and lasted for more than half an hour,
on the peaks of The Palace of Westminster from 4:50pm
where it remained for a whole day.
The nation was shocked
by the news of Our Leader's demise.
This was the first glow witnessed in the dozens of years
since our observations of the area started.

(xii)

A natural wonder was also observed
around the statue of the President
standing on Tonghung Hill
and near the statue of Churchill
in Parliament Square.
At around 9:20pm on Tuesday April 8
a Manchurian crane
was seen flying round the statue three times
before alighting on a tree.

(xiii)

The crane stayed there for quite a long while
in the branches of that bare tree
with its head drooped
and its wings lowered like flags

when the wind slows then falls away.
It flew in the direction of Pyongyang
from Parliament Square
at around 10pm.

(xiv)

Observing this
the director of the Management Office for the Hamhung
Revolutionary Site
said in unison
with the temporary leader of the British Conservative Party
"that even the crane
seemed to mourn the demise of Our Leader:
a crane born of Heaven
who flew down here at the dead of cold night,
unable to forget."

The Second Time as Farce

The men in orange and yellow striped lycra tights,
the men in fishnet stockings and white silk suspender belts,
are calling to the women wearing pink lace fairy wings,
the women wearing yellow *San Diego* cheerleader vests,

and the men in bottle-blonde Marilyn Monroe wigs,
the boys in animal masks borrowed from *The Wicker Man*,
are calling to the women wearing green leather basques,
the girls in cut-off denim shorts and cowboy boots,

and the men dressed in football shirts and velour jester hats,
the men dressed as Crockett and Tubbs from *Miami Vice*,
are calling to the women wearing *Blade Runner* retro-1940s hair,
wearing pencil skirts, red lipstick, scarlet fingernails,

and the men dressed as Batman and Robin, as Adam West and Burt Ward,
the men in clown suits, or wearing Primark suits and ties,
are calling to the women in red-framed plastic spectacles
whose hair is inflamed to *Dallas* heights or roughly dyed,

and the man wearing nothing but his blue cotton boxer shorts,
the men in gimp masks and burkhas and Biblical robes,
are calling to the women dressed as nurses and chambermaids,
the girl dressed as someone I think I met, once, back in nineteen eighty-six,

and the man in a rubber *Point Break* Richard Nixon mask,
the men in *Matrix* coats, in wide-brimmed black leather hats,
are calling to the women dressed in T-shirts that read: *'Frankie Says...',*
dressed as Toyah, Siouxsie Sioux and Cruella de Ville,

and the music that drifts from the windows of all the pubs
is by Eurythmics, by Whitney Houston and Adam Ant,
and the tinny music playing on every mobile phone
is by Grandmaster Flash, Five Star, The Smiths and Culture Club,

and they keep coming, gathered in groups of four or six,
to the epicentre of this Wednesday night, to Market Square,
to the open doors of Yates's, the two-for-one Jagerbomb carpet-bars,
the cocktail lounge where nothing's changed since 1993,

and in all this, between folk memory, amnesia and marketing,
the men in orange and yellow striped lycra tights
and the men in fishnet stockings and silk suspender belts
are still calling to the women wearing pink lace fairy wings.

Luigi Russolo

(for Alan Dixon)

Crank the handle, let these ratchets rumble and knock
like football rattles inside a plywood box.

Scrape a needle against this rough brass reel,
hear a sound like cold water on a broken wheel.

When an audience jeers, heckles and whines
I'll consider it a counterpoint to my noise-machines.

I'll rejoice in the echoes through a mountain pass
when startled horses gallop over a precipice!

This is the thunder gathering above a battlefield,
the sound of tank treads on a cobbled road,

the stammers and clatters of self-loading guns,
imagined explosions in heavy engineering zones!

I'd grasp the needs of a century, not yet amplified,
that will fear these sounds until it's hearing's freed.

But for now, I'll walk among the cones of church spires,
through the market squares where kettles hiss,

where butchers hammer at joints and bones, hooves clack
and clocks strike, awnings flap and geese honk,

voices burble and fires crack, wine glugs and onions spit,
the tiny maestro I keep under my black bowler hat

tapping his baton against the plates of my skull
like a roofer fixing thin slates to wood. There is skill

in this orchestration of things, poetry in the odours
of phenic acid and mercury, the burning sulphur

of a struck match, the whiff of sex on a whore's blouse,
the swish of mint in a park after the storms pass.

Arpeggios of speech! The arias of slaughtered cows!
Crescendos of steel! All these swift jigs of light in windows

that bounce from one side of any street to the other
while engines roar among the trees and changing weather!

The Shadow

    (after Angau, hen benillion, Welsh, c.1700 – 1800)

I couldn't rest for turning, all that night
the face of Death working hard at my sleep,

wind tearing strips from the lake's cold,
blowing curtains inward, though the sash was closed.

In the morning, dew lifting from the open fields,
I drew up basin and razor, clean white towels.

Yet before I'd wet the first pore of my skin
I caught Death's scent near me, lingering sweet

as the coal-tar soap and shaving cream
on the back of my hand. I felt myself weaken,

shivered, ran – away to the church in the village to pray
that I'd keep Death from me, live out that day.

But before I'd begun the first word of my prayer
I saw Death with a Bible, kneeling there.

From the lane, I heard him in the poplar's leaves,
in a farmer's coughing on an open field.

At the baker's, saw skulls in the shapes of a loaf,
at the butcher's smelt Death in a side of beef.

I passed by the porch of my brother's home
but his door was a stone in the mouth of a tomb.

I took a room at an inn, nailed shut window and door,
blew out all the candles, hid behind a chair.

No good, for – though I seemed secure –
Death rose like smoke through gaps in the floor.

I ran again, kept moving, my breathing short,
when a stranger, to whom I'd explained my plight,

said *'remember – old bones can neither fly nor swim'*.
I made for the ocean, thanks to him.

But as the land drew from me like a departing tide
and water glistened between quay and sky

I saw Death's silhouette cross the billowing sail,
knew his long white fingers had command of us all.

By Way of Digression

(or: Tearing Maps of Nottingham and Los Angeles into Small Squares of Roughly Equal Size, I Tape Them Back Together in Random Order, as a Single Mosaic Featuring Equal Parts of Both, and Try to Find a Way Back Home)

(for Frances Stark)

At the junction of Clumber Street and Market Square
I watch the ice-rink emerge from its scaffolding
as a cold fog clears. The sky's pale grey seems turquoise blue
when the dusk comes in and the lights turn on,
as Wilshire Boulevard becomes Woodborough Road,
Hollywood moves to Hollowstone and the paving slabs in Wellington Square
map a grid like the view of freeway lights
from Griffith Park inverted under their own steel moon.
Outside the Grauman's just off Heathcoat Street
I find marks on pavements, yellow paint,
angles and arrows, numerals, words,
lines from the Whitmans, Spillanes and Kerouacs
who rode the Big Wheel, went where they would
on City Rider cards to the outlands of Glendale and Warser Gate,
the deserts of Orange and Carlton Hill,
the all-night garages and cheap motels
of Long Beach, The Ropewalk and Spaniel Row.
Broad Street is Venice, where bamboo flourishes outside *Kayal*
and waitress-starlets take Chinese tea
in the street-facing windows of each café.
The billboards on Sepulveda Boulevard give us realtors,
Donuts, the Panto at Mansfield Palace Theatre,
a long wall of commercial print that runs from Radford to Rodeo Drive
as gutters freeze and the night grows deep. I keep moving,
take in the windmill at Watts, the Downtown dragon
with its stainless teeth, the Bath Street overlap with Beverley Hills
and crowded strip-lit Santa Monica bus

that stops at Victoria and Derby Road.
Pasadena nestles in a bend of the Trent,
its pueblos and semis, Aztec Hotels,
overlooked by the Clough Stand at Elysian Park.
Around Embankment and the County Hall,
deckchairs, rip-tides, the leaking heat
waxed into surfboards, stale bread broken for moorhens, swans.
I walk faster, from Echo Park to Wilford Bridge,
see pale moonlit sheets and lines of shirts
hung out on the cold. Somewhere between Hermosa Beach
and the lowered night barriers of Colwick Park
headlamps slice red-sandstone cliffs, throw long night-shadows
on the arterial roads linking Daleside
to the Pacific Coast. Pigeons are seabirds; an insect swarm
is dispersed in the glittering depths of space,
a constellation sharpened to punctuation-marks
pricked through indigo carbon sheets.
The first rays of sunlight float through cloud
like this idle thought – that I will find myself lost, or maybe
find myself, in Burbank, San Pedro or Lady Bay,
cross Euclid Avenue and Mulholland Drive,
the junction of Thoresby Street and St Stephen's Road,
my fingers like popsicles and both eyes closed.

Mnemonic to Aid Understanding of Public Debate Concerning the Fiscal Deficit

Remember that money doesn't grow on trees,
one must cut one's cloth to fit the bolt.

That nothing is free, or won unearned,
that sacrifice must concern us all.

That air is honey, pavements laid themselves,
that need is measured by what is sold.

That dogs are horses and blackboards wolves,
that red is white and both bleed blue.

That something is nothing and nothing all,
the moon a finger and each door a wall.

That cash is value and a heel a toe,
that bees are bottles and foot-stools globes.

That floors are windows, mirrors jewels,
coat-stands piglets and houses screws.

That what is isn't and what isn't is,
that a bathtub's a glacier and a tyre a rib.

That a vase is a cloud, a worm's a wheel,
that a horizon's a washing-line, a deal's a deal.

That a pump's a gourd and blood a gas,
that a flea's an elephant and a door-mat grass.

So remember: money doesn't grow on trees.
A whim's a hatchet and a stone's a seed.

Sonnets in the Aftermath and Anticipation of a Financial Meltdown

> "The world's an ark wherein things pure and gross
>   Present their lossful gain and gainful loss,
> Where ev'ry dram of gold contains a pound of dross"
> – Francis Quarles: *Emblems: Book II/VII* (1635)

(i) *Genesis*

What was brick is glass. What was solid glows
with a fire made visible among white shadows
at midnight. These are the streets we find ourselves on
as machines clean gutters and drunks head home
like victims of mustard gas stumbling over no-man's land
in the softening margins of nitrate film.
They lurch from street-lamp to alley, pavement
to wall, a carousel turning like a spinning plate
among the neon windmills and opaque signs
of Piccadilly Circus and Oxford Street. A slice of moon
floods the billboards reflected in shop façades
with sequins, skin tones, promised percentage gains.
Blown by the wind, no more than passing trade,
we cross a city someone else's money made.

(ii) *The Commandments*

What does money want? First of all, to exist,
to move from abstraction, take material form and test
our faith in its sway. It finds us wanting, builds walls,
sparks desire in the restless and insecure
as fear of the world outside money's sphere
lurks in the light-bulb shadows behind hot dog stalls
where nobody you'd want to meet would walk.
Office strip-lights, all-night cafés, a cathedral
whose bolts are drawn when the sun turns pale
and no key is turned till singing birds
have cleared the sky of every last shred of dark:
these are our bars, ourselves the guards.
Exits are points we neither conceive nor cross
though they stand wide open, where stones meet grass.

(iii) *A Prayer*

I shall never again take in vain the holy names
of the dollar, pound sterling or weakened yen.
I recant my heresy, for money renders all things of use.
I shall never more sin against nor blaspheme
the euro, rouble or offset package of mortgage CDOs.
I shall not write against finance, nor be the one
to say 'shit floats' when the parable of the rising cream
is invoked to explain the ways of cash to men.
Yea, for though the ways of money are unravelling,
too complex for containment by the human mind,
there are priests and wise men venturing
far offshore, casting prayers in all our names.
Should we now seek the blessing of money's friends
we must be silent and serve only money's ends.

(iv) *Revelation*

Will it be fear or relief that shows on your face
when your reflection hangs in the obsidian screen
of an ATM as all the networks finally collapse?
There may be flickering somewhere inside the machine
before all goes quiet and its lights blink out.
You might stand for a moment or whole long hour
in the hope that something might stir,
that credit and balances might flow again like light
before realising, when the world goes on (as it always does)
that nothing's changed. Taking down fences opens
but doesn't destroy a field; breaking chains
of zeros + ones leaves all they represent intact.
Remove the price-tags, strike down all records of profit and loss.
Every object and building will remain where it is.

On A Very Small Planet, Not Too Far Away

(i.m. Oliver Postgate, 1925 – 2008)

On a very small planet, not too different or remote from this,
small pleasures are shared, small problems solved
in garden sheds, over small brass cups of green tea
and in a spirit that perfectly comprehends
how small the very small planet is, how close its neighbours
in their iron nests and flimsy machines
of tinfoil and springs might be; how plants that sound with dew
or the white clouds from which glass beads fall
are all to be included and understood. When a boot kicks a door in
or a house is reduced to rubble, someone will help,
the whole story will hang on this, as a boy goes in search
of missing food, a train-driver travels miles out of his way
to drop a letter through a letter-box, neither profit
nor any return in mind; when a whole shop with a dozen staff
simply mends and returns those things thought lost:
this is a gift. This is a world we might promise ourselves
and begin to build, sipping our small brass cups
of green tea in allotment sheds, on balconies overlooking
new estates; a world where small pleasures
are always shared, small problems jointly solved
in a spirit that perfectly comprehends how small we are,
how close our neighbours, how necessary that spirit
glimpsed inside these small worlds, stop-motion manifestos
for a whole new kind of exchange, not utopian,
not concerned with power, but in acceptance of this once shared truth:
that when we wake, observe the cracks in this unknown thing,
we'll examine it, discuss it among ourselves,
work out how these fragments can be rebuilt, like new,
then, citizens of a state peopled by wood-peckers, mice, some folk musicians,
by soup-miners, chickens and marimba-leaved music trees,
by trains on uneconomic lines, by biscuit mills

pin-cushions and broken plates, by stairs of books
and vast fields of stars, by every kind of beauty and uselessness
this very small planet, not too remote from us, might yield,
we shall be awake, and yawn, and return to ourselves,
spring back from this washed-out sepia to our colour screens,
be human, fallible, content to lack any but the grandeur of small things
on a small blue planet, not so very far away from here.

A Cycle of Songs from the Body's Interior

(i.m. Minnie Betty Trueman, 1923 – 2012)

Panis et Circensis (Bread and Circuses)

(after Caetano Veloso/Gilberto Gil, 1968)

I wanted to sing a song of illumination,
shine sunlight on the sails I'd tie to masts,
the lions and tigers I'd let loose in yards –
but these people in the dining room
are too busy being born and dying.

I'd forge a knife from raw steel and glass,
make a sacrifice of my only love
when the clock strikes five on Central Avenue –
but these people in the dining room
are too busy being born and dying.

I'd dream of leaves in the garden of a house
where roots know to look for the rain
and stems reach for the sun at its height –
but these people in the dining room
are too busy being born and dying.

(i) *The Leukocytes*

Think of them as an Old Testament tribe,
a sect mentioned only once,
an apparition rising
like a cloud of flour from a slapped stone
in a marginal verse
on the purity of blood
and the ritual baking of bread.

(ii) *The History of the Red Cells*

They are the blood's red static,
plump oxygen wheels,
small bubbles of air
in a river whose currents
rush like sap, like wine,
between the boughs of lungs
and the heart's root,
bear all that's needed
to the place in need.
They are the blown leaves
of arterial trees
for whom whole seasons pass
with one drawn breath.

(iii) *The Origin of the Heart Beat*

This is your gravity's pull
on my heart's falling stone,
a fist that clenches, unclenches,
around a red copper coin.

(iv) *Electrical Changes in the Heart*

Between my heart's ripest fruit
and my lungs' wind-bent shrubs,
my breastplate's cracked shield
and that ache in my ribs,

I've installed a tiny pane of glass,
to show the world this chaos you cause
when you blow through the garden
of my bowed flesh and bone.

There, in the very instant you look,
you'll see each muscle flushed with dark,
all my flesh overcome by your kiss
like shaken cells, arterial grass.

(v) *Perfusion of the Excised Heart*

Light through torn cloth, glass arteries traced
on a window where condensation beads.
A flowering geranium warms blue light,
its red fist raised clear of a yellow cage of leaves.
There are lambs' hearts gleaming in cellophane,
dark pears staining a butcher's hands,
an arrhythmic pulse in a suspended web on pale air.
Things end. Light skips on water, is stone.
A meteor sparks on the raw edge of a static moon.
Thin curtains strain against the weight of dawn.

(vi) *The Circulation*

Take a seat by the window. Listen to this.
I'll recall the journey of an ordinary day
from a path among geraniums
and foxglove-spikes
to a stone-built post office
in a village street;
from the clatter of milk bottles
in a stopping electric cart
to your final long look
through the endlessly scattered stars of night.
Your nightdress is brambles
and wide-eyed owls,
your wallpaper ivy and holly vines.
In the dawn's blue haze
while half asleep
you'll feel the white noise
of blood in your veins,
sense the static of nebulae and galaxies,
the mutation of cells
and background collapse of stars,
touch the chill of sunrise
on a window's glass.
Take a seat by the window. Listen to this.

(vii) *Skin Sensations*

The soft abrasion, scrape of skin on stone
when you hit the ground –
then a raw plush of knuckle
as the healing bruise
deepens from crimson to midnight blue.

(viii) *The Lachrymal Apparatus*

The sun is written white, a blurred full-stop
pierced through broken clouds at noon,
a miraculously intact albino yolk
rolled in sugar and sifted flour on a marble plate.
Its iris burns among daylight stars
where a hesitant, mithering drizzle starts.

Water shines in the cracks of a fractured slab,
a fern stoops to touch black soil.
A bucket tests the whole sky's weight
in a convex mirror strewn with hawthorn leaves.
A radar-array of honeysuckle flowers
tracks an arc from here to the brink of night.

(ix) *The Properties of Nerve*

Dark rain encircles a stubble field,
straw fires are shorted by lightning strikes.

Here are brambles, labyrinths of open walls,
a Volkswagen left in a hedge to rust…

Nothing moves but a running fox,
a carrier bag caught on a barbed wire fence,

water rushing from a fractured pipe,
a mesh of shadows beneath one bare tree.

In the car park, a knife of broken glass
sparkles in darkness, like snow on moss,

a cigarette lighter running out of gas
whose flint rasps but makes only sparks.

(x) *Nerve Regeneration*

A net is cast, drags its knotted graph of ropes
through an offshore shoal, a flare of sun the lake reflects.
Wriggling scales and razor-fins are hauled into air.

What glitters next is a synapse flash, a gleam of thought,
a needle that pulls torn and severed mesh so tight
no kind of fish – not even the light of stars – escapes.

(xi) *The Peripheral Nerves*

Those who join house to house, field to field,
muscle to muscle and hand to eye,
may rewire the body to their own demands.
No good can come of this.

Houses lie deserted, fingers refuse to move,
good tendons are left to atrophy.
An acre of vineyard yields one glass of wine;
a wrist no longer turns.

(xii) *The Endocrine System*

These are continents of secretion among tides of breath,
ovarian pebbles, a pituitary stone, the kidneys' smooth
and fine-grained curves nestled in the lea of each lower rib.
Their hormones foam and scatter like dandelion seeds,
flow into blood, wash through every shifting mood,
float downstream like painted skiffs entering tributaries
on the Nile: *Permissiveness, Synergism, Antagonism.*

(xiii) *The Semicircular Canals*

I woke this morning with the word 'oursins'
and France Gall singing *Bébé Requin*
on a loop in my head. I'm listening,
I know, to a song with no source, a girl's voice
whose sound no longer disrupts the air
but circles somewhere inside the skull
as interference in this empty house
where I, still barely tuned, descend the stairs.

(xiv) *The Primary Organs of Sex*

The links in a pattern, one fold of white cloth,
this sheaf of dropped flowers and wet lace
in some empty room where light moves,
leaves flicker inside a window-frame,
a ladder leans to its own shade on a steel hook
and a warm bottle falls to the crease
of an open book, spills wine, stains a page
among breadcrumbs and grape-stems,
tissues and butter-smeared mobile phones,
scattered coins and deserted clothes,
late sun and the grass-scent of abandonment
in a sprung hollow where nothing lasts,
or needs to last, as long as this is all there is.

(xv) *The Physiology of Reproduction*

Imagine the almost imperceptible purr
of an amplifier before the music starts,

the low whine of incandescent bulbs
as steam expands inside a summer room.

Think of the hairs on your forearm
when they lift like grass in an open field.

Imagine these frequencies drifting,
a muscle tightening, a nerve-cell's blink

when some sensation occurs to skin
then registers in the brain or groin –

each live pore is one exposed red wire,
its small charge palpable in a fingertip.

Imagine raw meat strung from copper thread,
tendons strained as warm flesh glides –

daisies and ostrich grass, bent or stretched
where a star vibrates, a pulse shifts,

or something slips through air so moist
blue algaes and blooms of plankton swarm.

(xvi) *Pregnancy and Parturition*

A pale sky streaked with aircraft-trails, a garden
wired with filaments and trailing roots,

an assemblage of organs, soft bones and fluids
whose cells open, expand in the red shine

of a womb-wall when the seasons change
and blue light gleams on a wing-tip or a fuselage

while the sun's exposed. The breast fills,
body slows to a shallow breathing pace,

winds down to rest as its own weight grows,
turns a garden wired with filaments and trailing roots,

a new sky streaked with aircraft-trails
as old skin with scars, wholly upside down.

(xvii) *The Quadrants of the Breast*

The nodes are discovered like grapes in the wilderness:
the flesh is palpated with the flat of one hand,
sectioned in quarters like the bare ground
on which you build your house.

As with the first fruit of a fig tree in its first season
the fixity of cyst to skin, as fruit to bough,
surrenders to a gentle pinch of loose flesh
around this dark knot at the aureole.

So mapped, what is known as benign or threat, carcinoma
or neutral fluid, among the sixteen open ducts
that flow from this warm flesh into the air
one palm contains, may yet be judged.

(xviii) *The Deep Layers*

Leaves turn on the path, grass grows white with frost
where a hospital entrance breaks this cold horizon
on the edge of a car-park. You are contained here,
suspended high among saline drips and morphine shots
where tube-lights flicker on the fourth floor,
the cold scent of antibacterial fluid steeped in your hands.
We have seen all this before, know the grey linoleum
and white ceiling tiles, those cleansed sheets
folded back on empty beds. We know this is all to come.
For now, the doors slide open at our slow approach
and leaves turn over and over, speckled beige with damp,
foxed pages the acids of skin stain through.

(xix) *The Arterial Pulse*

Ask a clockwork bluebird, a sparrow built
from flywheels, cogs and eiderdown
what it means to breathe.

Do you feel a twitch at play in your wrist,
a red line charged in that musculature
like an electric wire?

Cogs might animate those wings and beaks
for ten or fifty or a thousand years
without a single breath.

All the crimson machinery beneath our skins,
the liquids carried among our bones –
in skin and sweat gland,

heart and groin – with careful maintenance,
low key repair, might break just once,
but fatally, in eighty years.

Ask a clockwork bluebird, a sparrow built
from flywheels, cogs and eiderdown
what it means to breathe.

(xx) *The Cortical Structures*

There was a grey wash of light, a screen of bare trees.
The world peeled back like a banner of skin
on a dissection plate, silver on a tarnished mirror
that flakes away, one glittering piece at a time,
to expose the ochre under-paint. There was an ice-field,
waterlogged, frost-white – hemmed in by pines.
There was a lake frozen like a cracked glass
on someone's bathroom shelf. You'd see foxes,
sometimes, through the cold birch wood.
There were twigs on snow like crackled glaze,
swans' feathers on a riverbank. She tested gas masks once,
knew girls in tiny rooms above Station Street
whose faces turned pale beneath asbestos dust.

(xxi) *Examination of the Tongue*

There is no obvious lesion, though leukoplakia
may render the surface white, like cracked emulsion paint.
In doubtful cases, press the tongue's root with a glass slide.
Note how the epithelium thickens, how the voice fades
to a small prayer carried on some scorching wind.
Each breath sands raw the crimson palate's
whole swollen nave. You might dream of the Atlantic
French-kissing a slate cave, pebbles clashing in flows of surf
like stone teeth; its wet tongue withdraws, returns,
withdraws, returns, while salt currents pull and words fail.

(xxii) *Supplementary Physical Signs*

I shall go now into this body of mine
and close these eyes behind me,
hide here for however long it takes
for the storm to pass.

Those palpitations in the clouds
may keep a regular, metronomic beat
or swerve abruptly to arrhythmias.
I'll wait until it's quiet.

(xxiii) *The Degeneration of Tissue*

Late spring afternoon. Dark trees hold their useless fruit.
Boughs drip and lean, heavy with light after hours of rain.

A blanket creases on a bed's steel frame. Her ribcage moves.
I hold five fingers in a loose skin glove nothing keeps from bone.

Her breathing ebbs in a sterile room where no-one speaks.
Strip-lights glare. Condensed grey mist on a window streams.

(xxiv) *Disorders of the Heart*

When I saw how ill she had by this point become
and she, in her part, saw how I was wounded at this,
then she turned to the great glass window
and looked across the motorway at the fields of Derbyshire,
their green intensities veiled by persistent rain.
But neither they nor I had power to cure this sickness
nor her thin hand any sway over that wound of mine.
I am no longer a young lion in my grandmother's house.
I am halfway myself to this meeting-place.
The days are unravelling. Cold dusks meet noons.
Red foxes drag carrion from black hospital bins.

(xxv) *The Coats of the Eye Ball*

This is the clarity that stops warm breath at noon
when a low sun's shadows recede like grass.
The ice takes over, each puddle a lens,
each infill of rain and brimming glass leaf
a corneal implant in the eye of things
beneath a clouding of frost. To have seen is enough.